Full of Beans

Henry Ford
Grows a Car

Peggy Thomas

Illustrated by
Edwin
Fotheringham

CALKINS CREEK
An Imprint of Highlights
Honesdale, Pennsylvania

Henry Ford made cars.

Millions of cars.

But this story isn't about cars. Well . . . maybe just one.

It's about one car and a lot of beans.

Henry had a mind for machines and was driven to improve the world around him. When he was young his mother said, "Do something useful," and encouraged him to make life for others a little smoother, a little easier, and a little happier.

Sometimes he was successful.

He built a smoother ride in his affordable Model T. (Sort of.) He sped up factories with the moving assembly line and made the workers happier with a five-dollar-a-day wage.

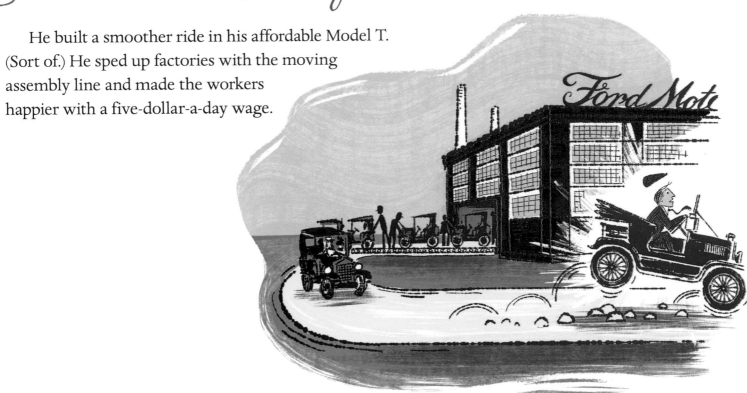

Sometimes he was not.

When he experimented with shrink-proof wool, all he got was a drawerful of tiny socks.

But one concern needled him his whole life. Farming.
Farming was hard work. No one knew that better than Henry.
Growing up on a Michigan farm, he dreaded the long hours behind
a horse and plow.

"*From the time I left that front gate as a boy . . . my only interest in a farm has been to lighten its labors. . . . If I can do that I shall have rendered a real service to humanity.*"

As a teenager he hammered together a crude tractor. But it couldn't haul a hayseed.

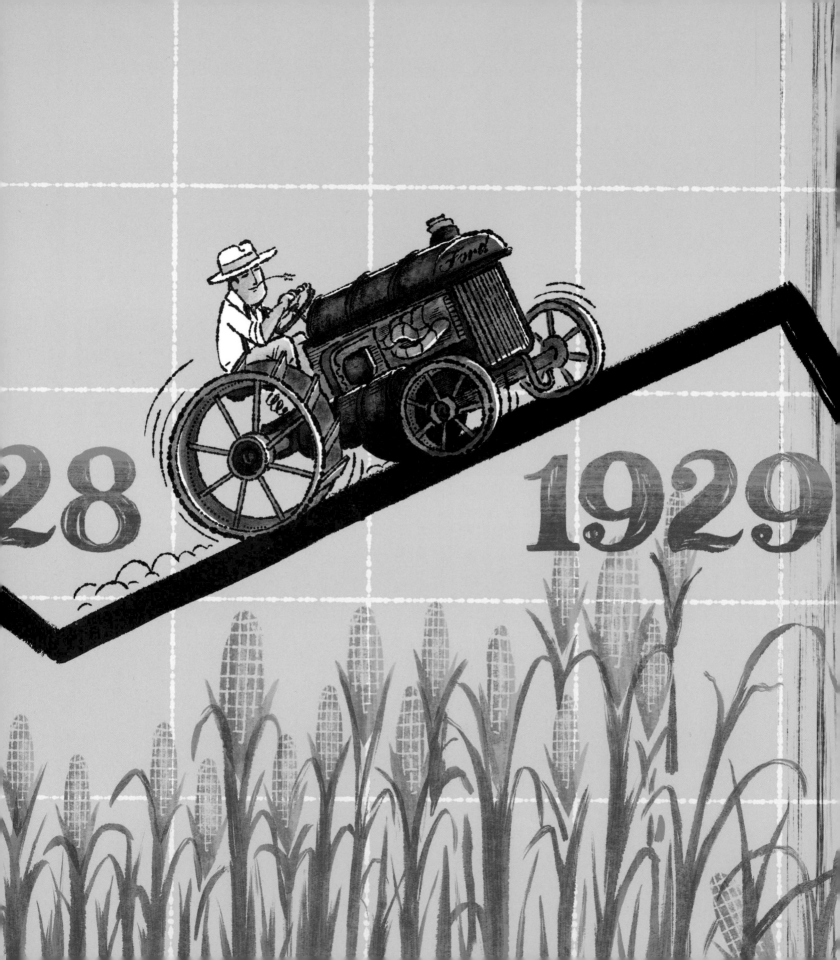

As a successful car manufacturer Henry still experimented with building tractors from leftover car parts. One of these tractors—the Fordson—sold for more than fifty years.

But heavy hauling and long hours of plowing was only part of the problem farmers faced. In 1929, the entire country suffered in the Great Depression. The stock market crashed. Businesses failed. People couldn't find jobs. Some farmers lost their land. Others left crops rotting in the field because they couldn't afford to harvest. Henry remembered his mother's words— "Do something useful."

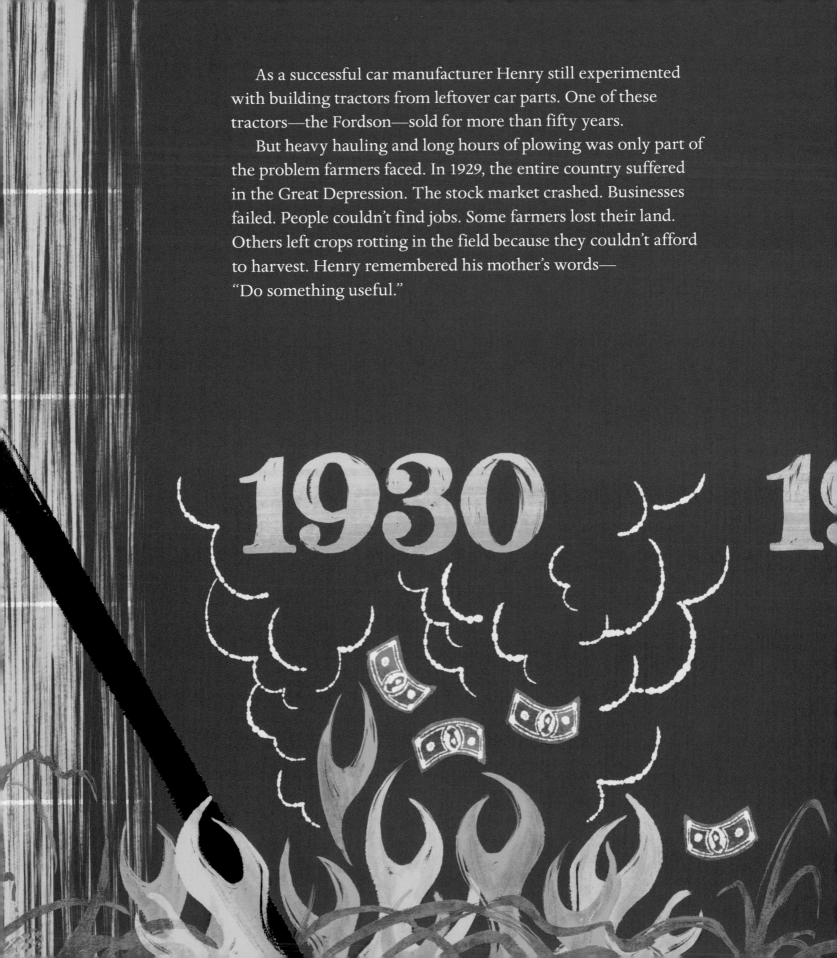

1930

What if farmers had a new market for their produce? They could earn more money, and their crops wouldn't go to waste.

Henry absolutely hated waste.

"Industry owes it to society to conserve material in every possible way."

Henry recycled everything. The Ford factory in Dearborn, Michigan, reused rags, boxes, and even sawdust. Every day, garbage trucks dumped seven tons of trash at the

factory, where it was processed and turned into useful products—fuel for cars, material to pave roads, fertilizer for plants, and charcoal briquettes for grilling hot dogs.

What if he used farmers' crops the same way?

"Anything that can be grown for industry's raw materials will bring new revenue to agriculture."

But first Henry had to figure out which vegetables were suitable.

On a patch of land that he called Greenfield Village, Henry built a laboratory. He hired a team of young men to study the chemicals in every grain, fruit, and vegetable. One of those men was Robert Boyer. While ratchets and widgets cranked and spun in Henry's brain, Robert thought about chemicals and atoms that could be pulled apart and mixed together.

Soon truckloads of vegetables tumbled in a heap outside the lab. Carrots one week, cornstalks the next. Turnips, tomatoes, and wheat. Robert ground, whirled, boiled, and stirred. Henry rocked or did chin-ups on a beam. (That was his way of thinking.)

After two years, they discovered the perfect crop for the factory . . .

People in China had grown and eaten soybeans for centuries, but in the United States the soybean was cow feed. To Henry it was a wonder crop. Soybeans were easy to grow, enriched the soil, and were bursting with oil and protein. Henry imagined farmers all across the country growing soybeans for food and for industry. But exactly what could they make from the oil and protein of the little legume? To work that out, Henry needed lots and lots of soybeans.

In the spring of 1932, a fleet of Ford tractors planted three hundred different kinds of soybeans across eight thousand acres. Soon the city of Dearborn sat in a sea of soybeans.

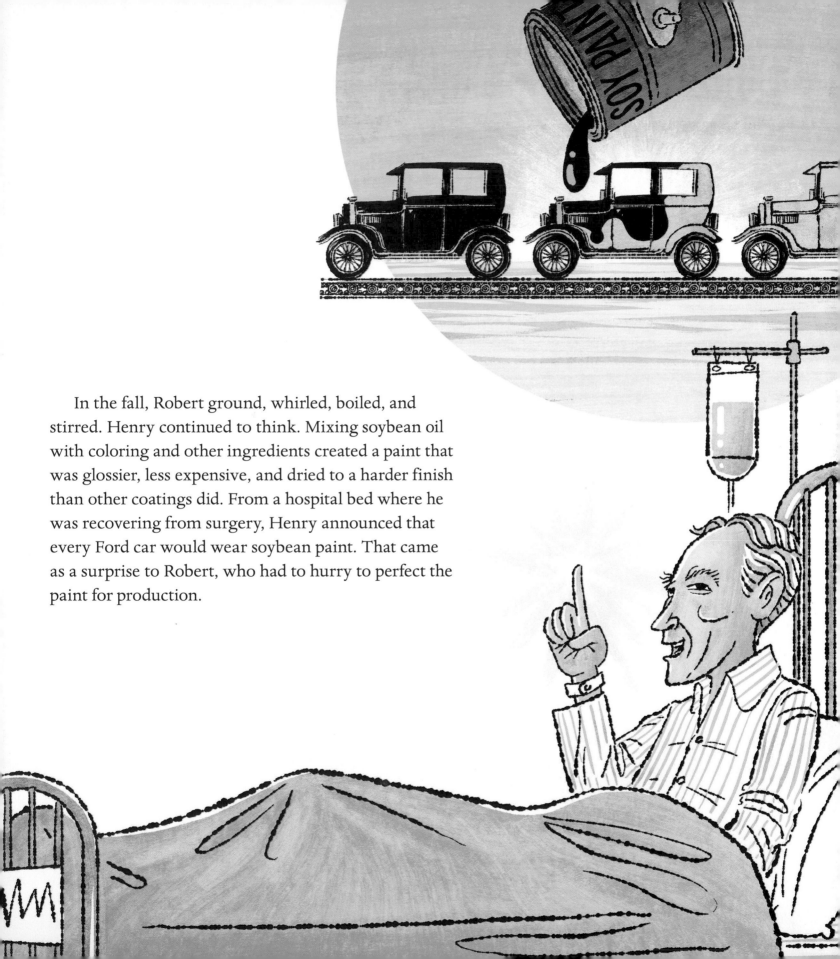

In the fall, Robert ground, whirled, boiled, and stirred. Henry continued to think. Mixing soybean oil with coloring and other ingredients created a paint that was glossier, less expensive, and dried to a harder finish than other coatings did. From a hospital bed where he was recovering from surgery, Henry announced that every Ford car would wear soybean paint. That came as a surprise to Robert, who had to hurry to perfect the paint for production.

Next, Henry's team mixed soy protein with a chemical resin to make a hard plastic. Soon cars rolled off the assembly line gleaming with soybean plastic horn buttons, gearshift knobs, light switches, and distributor caps.

The more cars Henry built, the more soybeans he needed. Henry kept a network of seven hundred Michigan farmers busy growing more than twenty-two thousand acres of soybeans.

Some people thought Henry was full of beans. And he was.

He ate beans.

One of his favorite snacks was the "Model T," a soybean cracker cut from the dough using a real Model T hubcap. Henry sold soy flour to factory workers and served soy ice cream in the lunchroom.

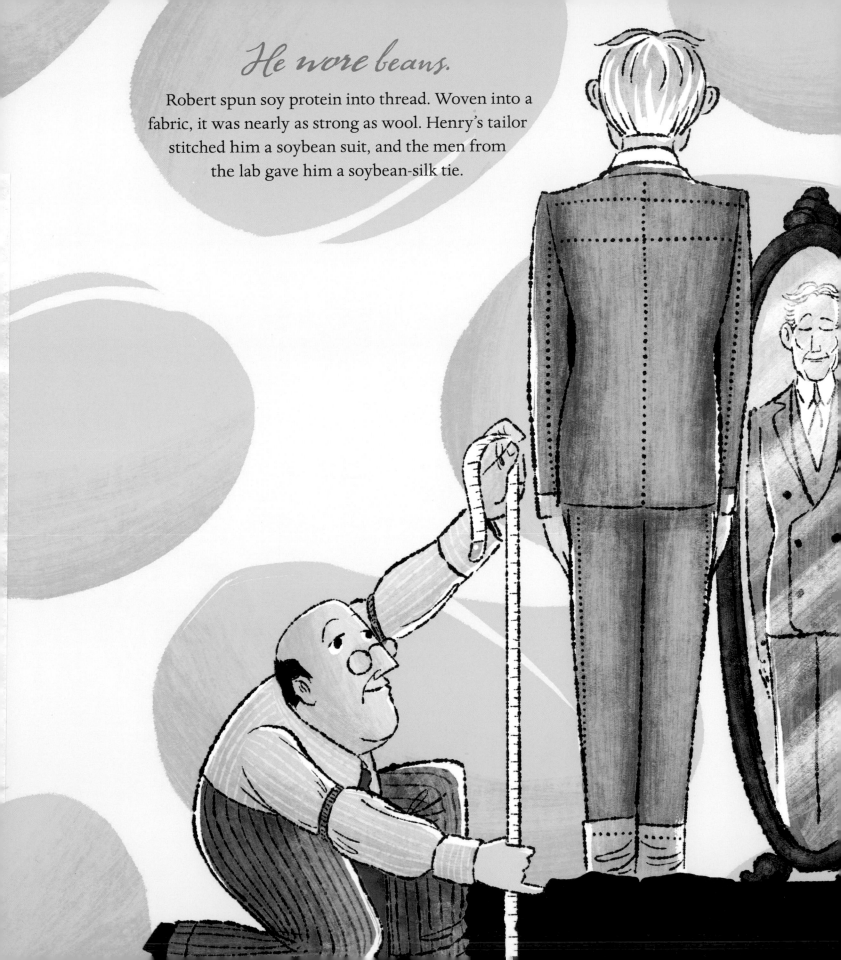

He wore beans.

Robert spun soy protein into thread. Woven into a fabric, it was nearly as strong as wool. Henry's tailor stitched him a soybean suit, and the men from the lab gave him a soybean-silk tie.

And Henry wanted to *drive* beans.

Every Ford car already contained a bushel of soybeans, from the gearshift knob to the paint. But Henry wanted the cars even beanier. He imagined an automobile as revolutionary as his Model T. A whole car made out of soybean plastic, so lightweight it would use less gas than any other car on the road.

Making small plastic parts was easy. Molding giant plastic panels was not.

When the first panel popped out of the mold, Henry grabbed his ax. Aiming the blunt end, he swung.

Thwack –crack!

He punched a hole clear through.

To test the strength of the next panel, Henry jumped up and down on it. "If that was steel," he said, "it would have caved in."

Henry attached a plastic trunk lid to his own car. With a crowd of people watching, Henry opened the trunk and pulled out his ax. He swung as hard as his wiry frame would allow. This time the ax bounced off the plastic and over his shoulder.

It was time to assemble the car.

Henry's team affixed the plastic panels onto a tubular steel frame. Two fenders in the front, two in the rear, a front grille, the engine hood, the doors, and a roof. Fourteen plastic panels in all. No one had seen anything like it. The men in the Ford plant called it a monstrosity, just an old man's hobby.

Henry knew it was much more. It wasn't just a car. It was the perfect symbol for how farms could fuel factories.

On August 13, 1941, everyone gathered for the Dearborn Day festivities. Dressed in his soybean suit, Henry rode to the fairgrounds in his sleek new automobile the color of a wax bean.

Some folks joked that the car ran on salad dressing rather than gas.

Others saw Henry's revolutionary vision. "Please hurry it," one reporter wrote. "Mr. Ford; hurry, hurry!"

But four months later no one was talking about Henry's amazing soybean plastic car. On December 7, the Japanese Navy attacked Pearl Harbor, and America was at war. The Ford Motor Company stopped making cars and began building bomber planes. The soybean plastic car rolled into storage. Nobody knows for sure, but its steel frame may have been recycled for the war effort. The plastic panels disappeared.

It would be one of Henry's last innovations. He died on April 7, 1947.

Henry will always be remembered for making cars.
Millions of cars.
 But only one proved that Henry was *not* full of beans.
Today soybean farmers continue to fuel factories—
 growing furniture and flooring,
 dog biscuits and bread,
 candy, crayons,
 and cars.

Henry Ford tests his "automobile plow" tractor on his farm in 1907.

#1 U.S. Soybean Man

Henry is famous for founding the Ford Motor Company in 1903 and for building the Model T, which changed America from a horse-and-buggy country to a nation of paved roads. In 1913 Henry sped up production by introducing the moving assembly line, and in 1914 he increased workers' pay to five dollars a day. Yet most people don't realize that Henry's work with soybeans had just as much impact on American society as his work with cars. *Time* magazine called him "a bean's best friend" and "#1 U.S. Soybean Man" for his positive influence on agriculture and industry.

When Henry started experimenting in 1929, there were only three million acres of soybeans grown in the United States. His research increased demand dramatically, and today American farmers plant more than eighty-four million acres, making it the country's second-most-grown crop. (Corn is the first.)

Henry's work with soybeans was part of a new science called chemurgy. It's the study of chemicals inside everyday materials and how they can be used as building blocks for other products. The soybean was not Henry's only chemurgy project. In 1927 he teamed up with Thomas Edison and Harvey Firestone to find an alternative to rubber, and he experimented with different plant-based fuels. "The fuel of the future," Henry said, "is going to come from fruit like that sumach out by the road, or from apples, weeds, sawdust—almost anything."

Henry's soybean plastic car would have been the perfect showcase for what chemurgy could do, if it hadn't been for World War II.

Although the war stopped the car project, it helped develop soy foods. Scientists were looking for an alternative to meat and dairy, which were rationed. Henry's soybean team created non-dairy whipped topping from the oil, and Boyer created a vegetarian meat substitute from the protein. While making soy fiber, Boyer tasted the material to check if it was ready. That's when he realized he could mold and flavor the fiber. His first product was a soy pork chop that he created in his basement lab. Today, soy oil and protein are used in many prepared foods. The average American eats about half a cup of soybean products every day.

The Model T, 1908

Super Soybeans!

If you've ridden down any stretch of country highway, chances are you've seen a field of soybeans. In the summer the legume is a low crop of bright leafy green. Autumn turns the fields a bright yellow. One soy plant grows sixty to eighty fuzzy pods that contain three or four beans each. The beans are high in oil (eighteen percent) and protein (thirty-eight percent), making them especially useful in manufacturing everything from food to furniture (see the list below).

Soybeans, which originally grew in East Asia, arrived in the United States in 1765, when a British colonist named Samuel Bowen planted the first seeds in Georgia. Today the soybean grows in almost any climate, and like other legumes it works in partnership with *Rhizobium* bacteria to add nitrogen, a vital nutrient, to the soil.

Products That Contain Soybeans

Margarine	Cereal
Glue	Engine oil
Carpeting	Mayonnaise
Biodiesel fuel	Candles
Sunscreen lotion	Medicine
Cooking oil	Soap
Car wax	Tabletops
Cosmetics	Building materials
Rubber	Ink
Cleaning products	Cheeses
Baked goods	Furniture
Crayons	Fire extinguisher foam
Paint	

A soybean field

The Ford World Pavilion at the Century of Progress World Exposition in Chicago, 1934. Note the old barn on the left. After the fair, Henry moved the pavillion to Dearborn where it became a visitor's center until it burned in 1962. The barn was reconstructed in Greenfield Village.

Celebrating Soybeans

In 1934 Henry celebrated the soybean at the World's Fair in Chicago. He painted the mammoth Ford pavilion with soy-based paint, planted an acre of soybeans along one side, and moved his father's old barn from Dearborn to the fairgrounds to house a soybean exhibit. He even hosted an all-soybean banquet. But few diners shared Henry's love of all things soybean.

Menu of Dinner Served at Ford Exhibit
Century of Progress
August 17, 1934

Tomato Juice Seasoned with Soy Bean Sauce
Salted Soy Beans • Celery Stuffed with Soy Bean Cheese
Puree of Soy Bean • Soy Bean Cracker
Soy Bean Croquettes with Tomato Sauce
Buttered Green Soy Beans
Pineapple Ring with Soy Bean Cheese and Soy Bean Dressing
Soy Bean Bread with Soy Bean Relish
Soy Bean Biscuit with Soy Bean Butter
Apple Pie (Soy Bean Crust)
Cocoa with Soy Bean Milk • Soy Bean Coffee
Assorted Soy Bean Cookies • Soy Bean Cakes
Assorted Soy Bean Candy

Model T Crackers*

The baker who made Henry's favorite soy snack cut out the dough using a real Model T hubcap that was only two inches across. You can use a cookie cutter instead.

Ingredients

⅔ cup all-purpose flour

⅓ cup soy flour

1 tablespoon sugar

½ teaspoon salt

½ teaspoon baking powder

4 tablespoons soy margarine (or butter)

3 tablespoons soy milk

Directions

- Preheat oven to 350 degrees.
- In a medium-sized bowl, mix flours, sugar, baking powder, and salt. Add margarine, using a fork to chop it into pea-sized pieces. Add milk one tablespoon at a time. Work into a ball.
- On a floured surface, roll out dough to a thickness of ⅛ inch.
- Cut out crackers with a 2-inch round cookie cutter.
- Place crackers on baking sheet. Prick each cracker three or four times with a fork.
- Henry liked his crackers sprinkled with wheat germ before being placed in the oven. Experiment with a little salt, sugar, cinnamon, or sesame seeds.
- Bake 10 to 12 minutes or until edges are lightly browned.

*Ask an adult to help with anything sharp or hot.

Ford: Still Growing Cars

In 1936, the Ford Motor Company used 450,000 bushels of soybeans. Each car was reported to contain ten to fifteen pounds of soybean plastic, and five pounds of soybean oil went into the paint and the making of metal molds.

Some people claim the body of the 1941 plastic car contained few soybeans, but Lowell Overly, who designed the car, said soybeans were the main ingredient. The soy protein slurry was sucked up into vacuum molds and heated under high pressure. Other filler material may have included wheat, hemp, flax, and ramie. Sadly, no production notes survived.

Henry's idea of a plastic car was way ahead of its time. He knew that plastic would make a car lighter, so it would use less gas. It could also replace steel, which was becoming scarce due to the war. But Henry's car was only a prototype, a test model. When America went to war, there was no time to develop it further. After the war, plastic made from crude oil was cheaper and overshadowed the soy plastic.

Today, the soybean is once again an important part of car manufacturing. More than thirty-two thousand soybeans are used to make some of the three hundred pounds of plastic that go into every Ford, and all seats are filled with soy foam. Ford uses other crops too: cotton, flax, jute, rice, and natural rubber, as well as recycled materials.

Henry would be pleased.

Soy-based plastics could be molded into thick, hard sheets (1940).

The soybean plastic car frame, 1941

Make Your Own Soybean Plastic*

Ingredients

- 1 tablespoon cornstarch
- 1 tablespoon water
- ⅛ teaspoon soybean oil (vegetable oil)
- 1 wide-mouthed glass jar or cup

Directions

- Mix cornstarch, water, and soybean oil in the glass container.
- Microwave the mixture for twenty seconds.
- Carefully take the container out (it will be hot).
- Let cool, then scoop out your creation. The heat will have allowed the starch in the cornstarch to bind with the soybean oil to form plastic.

*Ask an adult to help with anything sharp or hot.

Full of Beans Timeline

1863–Born July 30 near Dearborn, Michigan

1882–Builds a homemade tractor

1902–Buys his boyhood farm

1903–Forms the Ford Motor Company

1908–Introduces the Model T, an affordable, easy-to-drive car

1913–Introduces the assembly line to speed up production

1914–Raises factory workers' pay to five dollars a day

1917–Sells Fordson tractors (until 1964)

1929–Creates chemical lab at Greenfield Village; Great Depression begins

1931–Chooses the soybean for further research

1932–Plants eight thousand acres of soybeans

1934–Uses soybean-based paint on cars for the first time; presents soybean exhibit at Chicago World's Fair

1935–Boasts that a bushel of soybeans goes into every car; hosts the first chemurgy conference in Dearborn

1936–Moves soy oil extraction from lab to Ford manufacturing plant at River Rouge

1937–Grows more than twenty thousand acres of soybeans in southern Michigan and processes twelve million pounds of soybeans

1940–Demonstrates the strength of plastic panels with an ax

1941–Introduces plastic car on August 13 in Dearborn, Michigan; United States enters WWII on December 7

1947–Dies on April 7, at age 83

Robert Boyer with models
of the soybean plastic car
and frame, 1941

Visit the Soybean Lab

Greenfield Village
20900 Oakwood Blvd.
Dearborn, MI 48124-5029
As you cross the railroad tracks just inside the Village gates, you'll see a tall gray building on the left. That is the original Soybean Laboratory. Walk inside and look up. The giant copper vat that used to hold tons of soybeans is still suspended from the ceiling. Off to the side is a replica of the six-ton machine that filled the entire first floor. It separated the oil from the protein meal. Henry and the soybean team worked in the little office upstairs.

For More Information

The Life of Henry Ford by The Henry Ford
thehenryford.org/exhibits/hf/

Soybean Ag Mag from Illinois Agriculture in the Classroom
agintheclassroom.org/TeacherResources/AgMags/
Soybean%20Ag%20Mag%20for%20Smartboard.pdf

The Soybean Car at The Henry Ford
thehenryford.org/research/soybeancar.aspx

Sources for Quotations

"Do something useful . . .": Edgar A. Guest, "Henry Ford Talks About His Mother." *American Magazine*, July 1923, p. 119.

"From the time I left . . .": Guest, p. 120.

"Industry owes it to . . .": Henry Ford with Samuel Crowther, *The Great To-day and Greater Future*. New York: Cosimo Classics, 2006 (originally published in 1926), p. 126.

"Anything that can be grown . . .": Arthur Van Vlissingen Jr. and Henry Ford. "Automobiles and Soy Beans: An Interview." *The Rotarian*, September 1933, p. 59.

"If that was steel . . .": Henry Ford quoted in David Lewis, "Henry Ford and His Beanstalk." *Michigan History Magazine*. May/June 1995, pp. 12–17. Vertical file: Soybeans, Articles, 1990s. Benson Ford Research Center, The Henry Ford, p. 13.

"Please hurry it . . .": David Lewis. "Henry Ford and His Beanstalk." *Michigan History Magazine*. May/June 1995, pp. 12–17. Vertical file: Soybeans, Articles, 1990s. Benson Ford Research Center, The Henry Ford, p. 13.

"a bean's best friend": "Little Honorable Plant." *Time*, vol. 28, no. 15, October 12, 1936, p. 80.

"The fuel of the future . . .": "Ford Predicts Fuel from Vegetation," *New York Times*, September 20, 1925, p. 24.

Research Materials

The Benson Ford Research Center in Dearborn, Michigan, contains most of the research material I consulted for this book. Especially enlightening were the oral histories—interviews of friends and Ford employees recorded more than fifty years ago. The Automotive Industry Design Oral Histories Collection and the Reminiscences from the Owen W. Bombard Interview Series can be accessed online at thehenryford.org. The interviews that I kept going back to were of Robert A. Boyer, Harold M. Cordell, J. L. McCloud, John Najjar, Lowell E. Overly, A. G. Wolfe, Rosa Buhler, and J. D. Thompson. William Shurtleff and Akiko Aoyagi at Soyinfo Center (soyinfocenter.com) have created an extensive bibliography and sourcebook of Ford's research as well as soy food through history.

Books

Bryan, Ford R. *Beyond the Model T: The Other Ventures of Henry Ford*. Detroit: Wayne State University Press, 1990.

Curcio, Vincent. *Henry Ford*. Oxford: Oxford University Press, 2013.

Ford, Henry, with Samuel Crowther. *My Life and Work*. Garden City: Doubleday, Page & Co., 1923. Accessed through Internet Archives at archive.org/details/mylifeandwork00crowgoog.

———. *The Great To-Day and Greater Future*. New York: Cosimo Classics, 2006. (Originally published in 1926.)

Lewis, David L. *The Public Image of Henry Ford*. Detroit: Wayne State University Press, 1976.

Simonds, William Adams. *Henry Ford and Greenfield Village*. New York: Frederick A. Stokes, 1938.

Skrabec, Quentin R., Jr. *The Green Vision of Henry Ford and George Washington Carver*. Jefferson, NC: McFarland, 2013.

Snow, Richard. *I Invented the Modern Age: The Rise of Henry Ford*. New York: Scribner, 2013.

Watts, Steven. *The People's Tycoon: Henry Ford and the American Century*. New York: Alfred A. Knopf, 2005.

Wik, Reynold M. *Henry Ford and Grass-roots America*. Ann Arbor, MI: University of Michigan Press, 1988.

Willemse, Jan, and Eleanor Eaton. *Cooking for Henry*. Virginia Beach, VA: Donning Co. Publishers, 1993.

Articles

Cameron, Don. "Reveals Scope of Plan for His Industrial University." *Detroit Free Press*, no date. Vertical file: Soybeans, Articles, Undated. Benson Ford Research Center, The Henry Ford.

Cruse, William T. "Ford and Plastics." Modern Plastics, vol. 17, no. 5, January 1940, p. 23.

"Economic Liberation for the Farmer." *Ford News*. June 1934, p. 108. Vertical file: Soybeans, Articles, 1930s. Benson Ford Research Center, The Henry Ford.

"Ford Predicts Fuel from Vegetation." *New York Times*, September 20, 1925, p. 24.

"Increasing the Use of Agricultural Products in the Automotive Industry." *Ford News*, 1935, p. 123. Vertical file: Soybeans, Articles, 1930s. Benson Ford Research Center, The Henry Ford.

Kresin, William. "From Soy Bean to Automobile." *Ford News*. May 1941, pp. 122 and 138. Vertical File: Soybeans, Articles, 1940s. Benson Ford Research Center, The Henry Ford.

Lewis, David. "A Bushel in Every Car!" *Ford Life*, May-June 1972, p. 14.

"Little Honorable Plant." *Time*, vol. 28, no. 15, October 12, 1936, pp. 76–80.

Lougee, E. F. "Industry and the Soy Bean." *Modern Plastics*, vol. 13, no. 8, April 1936, p. 13.

"Plastic Body Car Exhibited by Henry Ford." *The News-Palladium*, August 14, 1941, p. 7. Accessed at Newspapers.com.

Acknowledgments

I would like to thank the manager of reference services, Linda Skolarus, and her staff at the Benson Ford Research Center in Dearborn, Michigan. They never failed to find just the document I was looking for. Thank you to my editor, Carolyn Yoder, for her patience, and to the Henry Ford Heritage Foundation for helping me find Ford historian and author Henry Dominguez, who graciously read early drafts and shared his expertise, attention to detail, and thoughtful critiques with me. I am especially grateful to Amelia Miller from the Michigan Farm Bureau Promotion and Education Department for suggesting that I write about Henry Ford's farming. I thought she was crazy until I started to do the research and got hooked.

Picture Credits

Robert Boyer and Henry Ford with the soybean car, 1941

For Daniel and Carly
—P.T.

For my family
—E.F.

For information about permission to reproduce selections from this book,
contact permissions@highlights.com.

Calkins Creek
An Imprint of Highlights
815 Church Street
Honesdale, Pennsylvania 18431
calkinscreekbooks.com
Printed in China

ISBN: 978-1-62979-639-0
Library of Congress Control Number: 2018944555
First edition
10 9 8 7 6 5 4 3 2 1

The text of this book is set in Dante MT.
The drawings are digital.

PRINTED WITH
SOY INK
Trademark of American Soybean Association